W9-BOC-597

CIPHERS, CODES, ALGORITHMS, AND KEYS

CIPHERS, CODES, ALGORITHMS, AND KEYS

LAURA LA BELLA

ROSEN
PUBLISHING®

Published in 2017 by The Rosen Publishing Group, Inc.

29 East 21st Street, New York, NY 10010

Copyright © 2017 by The Rosen Publishing Group, Inc.

First Edition

Library of Congress Cataloging-in-Publication Data

Names: La Bella, Laura, author.
Title: Ciphers, codes, algorithms, and keys / Laura La Bella.
Description: First edition. | New York : Rosen Publishing, 2017. | Series:
  Cryptography : code making and code breaking | Audience: Grades 7–12. |
  Includes bibliographical references and index.
Identifiers: LCCN 2016017414 | ISBN 9781508173069 (library bound)
Subjects: LCSH: Cryptography—Juvenile literature. | Ciphers—Juvenile
  literature.
Classification: LCC Z103.3 .L25 2017 | DDC 005.8/2—dc23
LC record available at https://lccn.loc.gov/2016017414

Manufactured in China

222 1582

CONTENTS

INTRODUCTION

More and more of our daily life is digital in some way, from the way we communicate via smartphone, email, and texting to the way we pay for goods and services and access our bank accounts. These highly personal and sensitive pieces of information—our passwords, our bank account numbers, and more—need to be kept secret.

If you want to keep something secret, you have two choices: you can hide the information, or you can make the information unintelligible. Cryptography is the art and science of making information unintelligible and keeping information secure from unintended audiences. Cryptography is what ensures that our sensitive information is kept private.

Cryptography encompasses various ways to encrypt information. Each time you use an automated teller machine (ATM), buy something online, text someone with your smartphone, use a key fob to unlock your car doors, or use your password to access your email, encryption is at work protecting your data. Encryption takes any message and scrambles it in a way that makes it unintelligible.

Cryptography is used by nearly all organizations, both military and private. Our military and diplomatic forces use cryptography to keep confidential information from unauthorized eyes, especially those of foreign and antagonistic governments. Businesses and corporations send and receive sensitive data that has been encoded to try and protect all types of information, from trade secrets to your personal data. Cryptography is used by any organization that uses computers or a computing network to access, store, or communicate information.

Without even realizing it, encryption has become a daily part of our lives. With every password you type, you are using it.

There are a variety of ways to encrypt information. Ciphers, codes, algorithms, and keys all aid in hiding and masking text so that it can be sent safely to its intended audience.

Ciphers are a way to make a message secret by changing or rearranging the letters in a message. They can be simple and done using paper or and pen. Or they can be highly complex and use powerful computing software. Codes are a system of symbols that represent letters, numbers, or words. These are used to mask information and make it difficult for someone to understand your intended message. Algorithms are sequences of processes, or rules, used to encipher and decipher messages. They are complex mathematical equations that are impossible to complete without powerful computing software. Unlocking all of the information hidden by ciphers, codes, and algorithms are keys. A key is a variable that is applied using an algorithm, which is a complex mathematical equation, to a plaintext message to produce encrypted text or to decrypt text. You can think of a key as the secret piece of information that unlocks encrypted information. Without a key, the hidden information, however it has been encrypted, is useless.

Cryptography is the art of keeping information secure, whereas cryptanalysis is the science of breaking encoded data. Many cryptanalysts are highly educated mathematicians. The branch of mathematics encompassing both cryptography and cryptanalysis is called cryptology. This field is exciting and evolving quickly, and it offers exciting career opportunities. Understanding cryptography is the first step to getting a solid foundation in learning how encryption affects our daily lives.

CHAPTER 1
CRYPTOGRAPHY: A SECRET LANGUAGE

The National Security Agency (NSA) has been in charge of encryption systems for the US government since 1952, when the NSA was formed. The foundation of the NSA can trace its roots back to World War I, when codes and ciphers were used by many foreign countries to encrypt secret messages being sent from military leaders to their troops around the world.

Today, the NSA is an intelligence agency that is responsible for monitoring, collecting, and processing information and data on a global scale. They also protect our nation's communication and information systems. According to the agency's website, the mission of the NSA is to develop and manage outstanding cryptologic systems and tools, make sense of and secure electronically gathered information, and intensify national security systems and other crucial operations and data as needed.

While the vast majority of the NSAs contributions to the world of cryptography are classified and cannot be shared with the public, one of its most significant contributions to American security came during the Cold War, a long-standing political and military dispute that existed between the United States and the Soviet Union for more than forty years. The Verona Project was a secret program that began in February 1943 when cryptologists began working to break KGB (state security police in the former Soviet Union) encrypted communications being sent from the Soviet Union to the United States. The KGB was the main security agency for the Soviet Union from the mid 1950s until the break up of the Union of Soviet

Socialist Republics (USSR) in 1991. The Verona Project cracked encrypted information being sent to and from Soviet spies living in the United States. The project uncovered significant spy rings in the United States, espionage missions, and the identities of many Soviet spies. The Verona Project had hundreds of cryptanalysts working for forty years to decrypt more than three thousand Soviet messages. The Verona Project is a prime example of cryptography at work to ensure our national security.

WHAT IS CRYPTOGRAPHY?

Cryptography is the science of making information secure by using encryption to transform numbers, words, text, sounds, and images into a stream of unintelligible information.

Encryption surrounds us and makes it possible for us to do many of our day-to-day activities. For every call made on your cell phone, every purchase made in a store or on the internet, and every text message or email you send, an image of the information (cell phone numbers, credit card numbers, text messages, images, and more) is scrambled using encryption.

There are many ways to encrypt information. Some forms are simple while others are extremely complex. Most involve swapping letters for numbers and using mathematic algorithms to perform the transformation of comprehendible information into unintelligible data. Regardless of how the information is encrypted, the scrambled information should give no clues as to how it was encrypted. The "how" is the secret to maintaining the privacy and confidentiality of the scrambled data. Encryption secures

Every method of communication, such as e-mail, whether it is online or on smartphones, uses encryption to protect our conversations.

the information and makes it impossible for someone to understand it, unless they hold the key to decrypting it. Decryption is the process of taking the encrypted data and unscrambling it into its original, understandable form.

A HISTORICAL OVERVIEW OF CRYPTOGRAPHY

The study of cryptography, called cryptology, is a relatively new science that began about one hundred years ago. But cryptography can be traced back through history to as early as 1900 BCE, when the first known evidence of cryptography was found in an inscription carved in the main chamber of the tomb of the nobleman Khnumhotep II, in Egypt. Julius Caesar was known to use a form of encryption to convey secret messages to his army generals

A CAREER AS A CRYPTOGRAPHER

A cryptographer is someone who is skilled at analyzing and deciphering encrypted information or someone who can encrypt data to ensure its security. Positions as a cryptographer—which can also go by the following job titles: cryptanalyst, cryptologic technician, cryptologic linguist, symbolist, decipherer, information security expert, intelligence agent, or information security engineer—begin with a four-year bachelor's degree in computer science, mathematics, engineering, or computer programming. These degree programs are all heavily focused on mathematics. Most positions require a master's degree as well as mastery of additional subject areas, such as foreign languages, political science, and international relations.

Jobs are available in government agencies such as the Central Intelligence Agency (CIA) and the NSA, with all branches of the armed forces, as well as with large-scale corporations where the security of large amounts of sensitive information is necessary. These can include financial institutions, corporations, and health care companies. It's a growing field with above-average salaries and a range of growth opportunities.

during the war. His use of cryptography resulted in the Caesar cipher, the most talked about historic cipher in academic literature. Cryptography was heavily in use during World War I and World War II.

Modern day cryptography is crucial to our armed forces. It aids in national security, and its use became prolific beginning in the 1970s as a way to secure military information, including secrets gained through spying. Cryptography was soon seen as essential by businesses and corporations that needed to secure trade secrets and protect the personal information of customers. At the same time, the academic and scientific communities saw an increased need for cryptography when the computer revolution made computers as well as other devices, such as smartphones, laptops, and tablets, readily available to the public. This coincided with the explosive nature of the internet and changing ways people began to communicate and function in their daily lives. Cryptography enables secure electronic transactions, confidentiality of industry secrets, protection of our personal information, and secure wireless communications.

These needs have created an uptick in the call for professionals with the required skills to work for organizations as cryptologists and cybersecurity specialists. In the last fifteen years, academic

Julius Caesar recognized the importance of cryptography during his time as a general of the Roman Empire.

The Navajo Code Talkers

During World War II, military communications had become a problem for the United States and its allies. Japanese cryptographers had become highly skilled at breaking the military codes sent by the United States—to their troops as well as those of their allies. Many Japanese code breakers had been educated in the United States and had learned to speak English, which meant that as soon as they could break the code, they could understand it.

Philip Johnston was a civil engineer who was raised on the Navajo Indian Reservation with his Protestant missionary parents. He knew the Navajo language and also knew it was extremely complex. Based on inflections in one's voice, a single Navajo word could have as many as four different meanings. To a listener, the language also sounded incomprehensible. He also knew the language was confined to the Navajo reservation. Having read a newspaper article on military security and communication issues, Johnston began imagining a secret military code

Hundreds of members of the Navajo tribe joined the US military to help encode messages using their native language to deceive the Japanese at the height of World War II.

based on the Navajo language that could not be broken by the enemy. He took his idea to the military, and after a test run, numerous bilingual Navajos were recruited to serve in the US Marine Corps as communication specialists. Their code was unbreakable by the Japanese and other foreign military enemies.

programs at colleges and universities are now available in cybersecurity, which covers cryptology, encryption, computer hacking, cyber attacks, and more.

TYPES OF ENCRYPTION

The purpose of cryptography is to encrypt information to keep it secure. To understand how cryptography is used and why, it's necessary to understand the three main ways in which you can encrypt a message: symmetric encryption, asymmetric encryption, and hashing.

Symmetric encryption is when you take information, scramble it to make it unreadable, and later unscramble the information when it's needed. The sender as well as the receiver of the message needs the same key. The key is used by the sender to encrypt the message; the key is also used by the receiver to decrypt it.

Asymmetric encryption works exactly like symmetric encryption except instead of one key there are two. One key is used by the sender to encrypt the data, and a different key is used by the receiver to decrypt it. Asymmetric encryption is also called public-key cryptography. One key is public and known to everyone. The other key is private and known only to the party that needs it to decrypt the information.

Hashing takes information and creates a hash, or a string of data. All hashes share the same three properties: the same data will always produce the same hash; it is impossible to reverse the data back to its original information, and it is impossible to create another string of data that will create the same hash. Hashing is what's happening when you hear about a password being encrypted. Your email, for example, stores your password as a hash. When you enter your password, your email program can check the password by hashing it to see if it matches the hash it has on record as your password. If it matches, your email gives you access to your account.

All three of these forms of encryption require the use of ciphers, codes, algorithms, and keys. When you mix up or substitute existing letters, you are using a cipher. When you substitute one word for another word or sentence, you are using a code. An algorithm is a progression or group of rules that are observed in computations or other problem-solving processes, particularly by a computer. Modern cryptographic algorithms are too complex to be executed by humans and require advanced computing. A key is a bit of data that defines what an algorithm or cipher puts out. A key specifies the precise change from plaintext into ciphertext, or the other way around through decryption.

Chapter 2

CIPHERS

Ciphers have been used as exciting plot points in books and movies throughout history. In the movie *National Treasure: Book of Secrets*, the Playfair cipher is used to encode a clue for a treasure hunt. In *The Lost Symbol*, a novel by Dan Brown, Robert Langdon, a Harvard University professor of religious iconology and symbology, comes across an unfinished black stone pyramid with a cipher that is

Cryptography appears in many Hollywood films, such as National Treasure: Book of Secrets. *Codes and keys heighten suspense, hide plot clues in plain sight, and add excitement to the story.*

decrypted using the Pigpen cipher. The back cover of Brown's novel also has two codes that can be deciphered if readers use the Pigpen cipher from within the book.

In these examples of cryptography in fiction, secret messages are hidden using different ciphers. Ciphers are methods used to conceal a message and its meaning.

WHAT IS A CIPHER?

A cipher (also spelled cypher) is a way to make a message secret by changing or rearranging the letters in a message. Plaintext, which is what the original message is referred to as, is encrypted using a cipher, which can combine substitution and transposition to change the message's original letters with other letters, numbers, and symbols. What is produced is a secret, encrypted message, called ciphertext. Ciphers can be simple or extremely complicated. The more complicated a cipher, the harder it is for someone to decode the message.

For a cipher to be useful as a way to hide text there are several things that must be known to both the sender of the message and the person who receives the message. First, both need to know the method used to encrypt the original message. Second, the key used with the method must be shared to allow the plaintext to be both enciphered and deciphered. And third, both must be aware of the period of time for which the key is valid.

TWO MAIN TYPES OF CIPHERS

There are two main types of ciphers: substitution ciphers and transposition ciphers.

SUBSTITUTION CIPHERS

With substitution ciphers, letters are replaced, or substituted, throughout the message for other letters in an organized way. This is not a random substitution, but one that follows a pattern.

For example, a well-known substitution cipher is the Caesar shift cipher. Created by Julius Caesar, the dictator of the Roman Empire, Caesar used the cipher to send military commands to his army. To encrypt a message using the Caesar cipher the sender would replace each letter of the message with a letter a certain number of spaces down the alphabet. For example, with a shift of 1, A is replaced by B, B is replaced by C, C replaced by D and so on. So, for example, "ROSEN" would be encrypted to "SPTFO." Caesar

The Caesar Cipher Wheel is a simple, fun tool used to code and decode messages.

MAKE YOUR OWN CAESAR CIPHER

Want to send someone a hidden message only they can read? Let's create a cipher. To make a cipher, follow these simple steps to use the Caesar shift cipher to encrypt a message.

Write down each letter of the alphabet:
A B C D E F G H I J K L M N O P Q R S T U V W X Y Z
Select a number that will be used as the key. Let's choose five for this example.
Starting with the letter A in the standard alphabet, count five spaces to the right and write A underneath E, with the remaining letters looping around to start back under A. It should look like this:

A	B	C	D	E	F	G	H	I	J	K	L	M	N	O	P	Q	R	S	T	U	V	W	X	Y	Z
W	X	Y	Z	A	B	C	D	E	F	G	H	I	J	K	L	M	N	O	P	Q	R	S	T	U	V

Choose your message.
Example: THE CAT IN THE HAT

Locate the first letter of your message on the standard alphabet (T) and use the letter below it as the cipher letter (P). Translate your entire message using this method. It should look like this: PDA YWP EJ PDA DWP.

often rotated the alphabet by three letters, but any number from 1 to 26 (the total number of letters in the alphabet) works.

Another method of substitution cipher is based on a keyword. This method works by taking a word, let's use MOUSE, as the keyword. Using the standard alphabet, replace the first five letters with the letters M-O-U-S-E.

M O U S E

Then complete the rest of the alphabet in order following the last letter of your keyword. The last letter in our example is E. So you'd start the rest of the alphabet with F, and continue without repeating any of the letters used in your keyword.

A	B	C	D	E	F	G	H	I	J	K	L	M	N	O	P	Q	R	S	T	U	V	W	X	Y	Z
M	O	U	S	E	F	G	H	I	J	K	L	N	P	Q	R	T	V	W	X	Y	Z	A	B	C	D

This is now your substitution cipher to create a hidden message. Choose a message to encrypt using this keyword cipher. For example, the message BELIEVE IN YOURSELF would be encoded as OELIEZE IP CQYVWELF.

The Caesar shift cipher and the keyword substitution cipher are examples of mono-alphabetic substitution ciphers, where just one cipher alphabet is used. A more complicated substitution cipher is a poly-alphabetic substitution cipher, which uses more than one alphabet. An encoder, or person hiding the message, would make up two or more cipher alphabets using whatever techniques he or she chooses. Using those alphabets, a message would be encrypted, alternating between the cipher alphabets with every other letter or word. This method of encryption makes a message much more difficult to decrypt because the receiver must know which cipher alphabets were used to encrypt the original message.

TRANSPOSITION CIPHERS

The second type of cipher used is called a transposition cipher. In this cipher the letters used in the original message stay the same, but their order within the message is scrambled using a defined method. A simple transposition cipher is too write each word in your message backwards. So a message that says "GREEN EGGS AND HAM" might read "NEERG SGGE DNA MAH."

Transposition ciphers make ciphertext appear to be well encrypted, however, this is not a highly secure way of encrypting data. Because transposition ciphers do not change the letters in a plaintext message, or even attempt to alter the consistencies of the message, they can be easily decoded. However, transposition ciphers can be used as a foundation to make more complex and secure forms of encryption.

POPULAR CIPHERS

Ways to conceal information have existed for thousands of years. As simple ciphers became easier to decode, more complex ways of encoding and hiding messages became necessary. Here is a selection of ciphers that have been used to hide, encrypt, or encode secret or sensitive information.

Steganography is the art of hidden writing. Throughout history, it has been necessary to pass messages from one person to another in secret ways to avoid detection. The best steganography uses everyday objects as vessels to carry messages. For example, in England, using newspapers was a popular way to hide and deliver information. Tiny dots made underneath letters used in a news story on the front page indicated which letters should be used to spell out a message.

ROT 1 is short for "rotate 1 space." It is a simple cipher that uses a very easy key: rotate the alphabet by 1 letter. Following this key, A is replaced with B, B is replaced with C, and so on. The message "BATMAN IS THE BEST SUPERHERO." becomes "CBUN-BO JT UIF CFTU TVQFSIFSP." ROT ciphers can be fun because they are easy to understand.

In the **Vigenère** cipher, the key to decoding a message is a word. The idea is similar to the Caesar shift cipher except each letter is decoded based on each letter of the keyword. If you use a keyword such as CHAIR, the C cipher alphabet is used to encode the first letter of a message, the second uses the H cipher alphabet, the third uses the A cipher alphabet, and so on. The word CHAIR is only five letters long, so to continue decoding a message, begin with the first letter of the key word again. So the sixth letter that needs to be decoded would use the C cipher, the seventh letter would use the H cipher, and so on.

The **public key cryptography** cipher is the most modern of our time and has

```
  A B C D E F G H I J K L M N O P Q R S T U V W X Y Z

A  A B C D E F G H I J K L M N O P Q R S T U V W X Y Z
B  B C D E F G H I J K L M N O P Q R S T U V W X Y Z A
C  C D E F G H I J K L M N O P Q R S T U V W X Y Z A B
D  D E F G H I J K L M N O P Q R S T U V W X Y Z A B C
E  E F G H I J K L M N O P Q R S T U V W X Y Z A B C D
F  F G H I J K L M N O P Q R S T U V W X Y Z A B C D E
G  G H I J K L M N O P Q R S T U V W X Y Z A B C D E F
H  H I J K L M N O P Q R S T U V W X Y Z A B C D E F G
I  I J K L M N O P Q R S T U V W X Y Z A B C D E F G H
J  J K L M N O P Q R S T U V W X Y Z A B C D E F G H I
K  K L M N O P Q R S T U V W X Y Z A B C D E F G H I J
L  L M N O P Q R S T U V W X Y Z A B C D E F G H I J K
M  M N O P Q R S T U V W X Y Z A B C D E F G H I J K L
N  N O P Q R S T U V W X Y Z A B C D E F G H I J K L M
O  O P Q R S T U V W X Y Z A B C D E F G H I J K L M N
P  P Q R S T U V W X Y Z A B C D E F G H I J K L M N O
Q  Q R S T U V W X Y Z A B C D E F G H I J K L M N O P
R  R S T U V W X Y Z A B C D E F G H I J K L M N O P Q
S  S T U V W X Y Z A B C D E F G H I J K L M N O P Q R
T  T U V W X Y Z A B C D E F G H I J K L M N O P Q R S
U  U V W X Y Z A B C D E F G H I J K L M N O P Q R S T
V  V W X Y Z A B C D E F G H I J K L M N O P Q R S T U
W  W X Y Z A B C D E F G H I J K L M N O P Q R S T U V
X  X Y Z A B C D E F G H I J K L M N O P Q R S T U V W
Y  Y Z A B C D E F G H I J K L M N O P Q R S T U V W X
Z  Z A B C D E F G H I J K L M N O P Q R S T U V W X Y
```

cipher	V V V R B A C P
key	C O V E R C O V E R...
plaintext	T H A N K Y O U

To begin encoding a message in a Vigenère cipher, locate the intersection of the plaintext's first letter ("T") along the top with the key's first letter ("C") along the side. This identifies the cipher's first letter ("V").

multiple alternatives, making decoding very difficult if you don't have the keys. This cipher involves a public key and a private key. The public key is available to everyone and is used to encipher or encode a message. The private key is known only to the receiver and is used to decode or decipher the message. The message cannot possibly be deciphered without the private key. This is a very secure method of encrypting data and is used by financial institutions to scramble your credit card information and other personal data.

CHAPTER 3
CODES

When you use your smartphone to scan a quick response (QR) code you're deciphering the code's message and learning its content. QR codes can be seen almost everywhere—on movie posters, in magazines and catalogs, on television, in department stores, and even on the web. QR codes direct audiences to specific information that the code keeps hidden unless you have a code reader on your smartphone. The code reader deciphers the code and follows the code's message, which can send you to a website, initiate a phone call, produce a web URL, connect to a Wi-Fi network, get coupons, and more. A QR code is a symbol

A QR code uses your smartphone as the code reader. It's a modern-day take on using technology to hide and uncover messages left in plain sight.

that contains various sizes of boxes. These boxes contain information that, once deciphered, produces a hidden message.

What Is a Code?

Many people think of codes as secret messages, like a code word in a spy movie that grants permission to an intelligence agent to enter a secret location. But in reality, a code is a system of symbols that represents letters, numbers, or words. Any word can be a code word. For example, the code word for a small, four-legged, furry animal that meows is C-A-T. Because you know those letters represent an actual cat, you know the code.

In cryptology, codes are necessary to make secret message. Codes change the words of your message into something else. For a message to be deciphered, a key is needed.

Some codes have practical uses for general communication. Morse code, for example, was developed when the telegraph was invented. It was a way for people to communicate over long distances. The telegraph allows a beep to be sent from the sender to the receiver, and Morse code translates those beeps, also called dots and dashes, into letters.

In Morse code, each letter has an assigned series of short or long beeps. A, for example, is one short beep followed by one long beep. B is one long beep followed by three short beeps. Messages were sent via telegraph, where each letter of the message was sent as a series of beeps, with a translator deciphering the message on the other end.

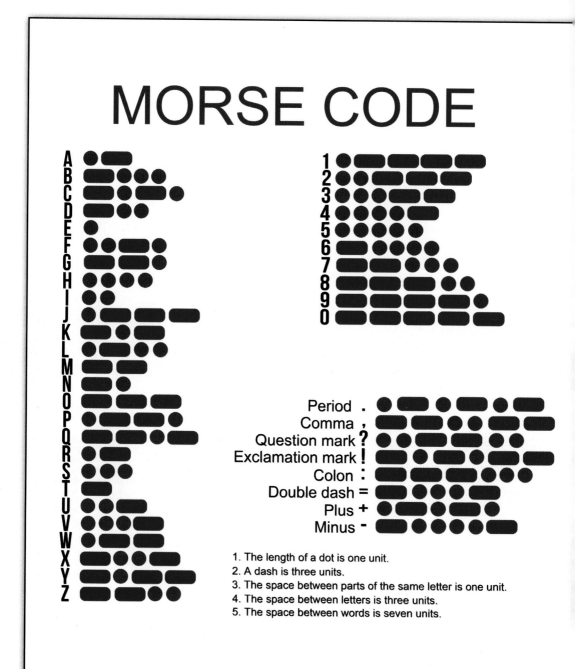

MORSE CODE

1. The length of a dot is one unit.
2. A dash is three units.
3. The space between parts of the same letter is one unit.
4. The space between letters is three units.
5. The space between words is seven units.

Morse code is still used today by naval pilots and others as a quick way to send and receive messages.

Morse code was widely used before the telephone and the radio were invented and became a chief way the military sent messages around the world. With modern communications, its use has significantly declined, however, it is still used today by the US Air Force.

THE KEY IS IN THE CODEBOOK

All codes need a key and the key is often found in a codebook. A codebook can be any type of document, such as a dictionary or a published book, which is used to help decipher a code. A codebook is used for two purposes: to encode a plaintext message by the sender and to decode the message by the receiver.

Say you want to code the following plaintext message: ONE FISH, TWO FISH, RED FISH, BLUE FISH. You need a codebook to encrypt the message. For this example we'll use a dictionary. Here are the steps you'd follow to encode your message:

1. Write down your plaintext message. ONE FISH, TWO FISH, RED FISH, BLUE FISH

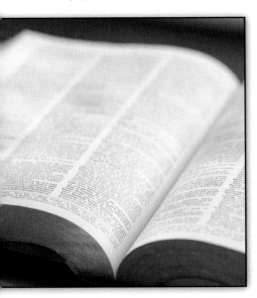

Any book, even your basic dictionary, can be used as a codebook to encrypt a message.

THE ZODIAC KILLER'S CODES

In the late 1960s, the Zodiac Killer was linked to at least seven murders and two attempted murders that were committed in Northern California. The killer sent messages to local newspapers that contained a symbol consisting of a circle with a cross through it. The letters also included a code that the killer claimed, once deciphered, would reveal his identity. The first code was a three-part cipher sent in portions to three local newspapers: the *Vallejo Times-Herald*, the *San Francisco Chronicle*, and the *San Francisco Examiner*. The complete cipher contained 408 characters and was published in the papers for the public to help solve. The code was cracked by a local history teacher, but it did not reveal the killer's identity. Numerous additional codes were sent to newspapers over the next several years, including one that has never been deciphered. This one was a 340-character cipher that was mailed to the *San Francisco Chronicle*. Even the FBI was called in and their cryptologists analyzed and attempted to decipher the code. The letters to local newspapers stopped in 1974 and to date, the killer's identity and the code of the 340-character cipher have not been discovered.

Not every code is fun to decipher. Some hide the names of murder suspects. The Zodiac Killer is still unknown, even after decades of expert attempts to decode his letters.

2. Find the first word of your message in the dictionary. You're looking for the word ONE.
3. Once you locate the word ONE, write down the page number where it appears, the column or paragraph, and the number of words you need to count to in that column or paragraph to arrive at your word. Page 1007, Column 2, Line 75
4. Separate the numbers using a period.
   1007.2.75
5. Repeat step 4 until the entire message is coded.
   ONE = 1007.2.75
   FISH = 534.2.62
   TWO = 1547.2.50
   FISH = 534.2.62
   RED = 1199.2.48
   FISH = 534.2.62
   BLUE = 159.1.58
   FISH = 534.2.62
6. The finished code for your message looks like this:
   1007.2.75 534.2.62 1547.2.50 534.2.62 1199.2.48
   534.2.62 159.1.58 534.2.62

The secret to deciphering a coded message is to know which source was used to encode the original message. This message was coded using a dictionary. But you can't choose just any dictionary or just any book. For this example, the *Webster's New World College Dictionary*, fourth edition, was used. If you use that version of the dictionary, you'll be able to decode the message. If you use another version of a Webster's dictionary, or a different dictionary altogether, you will not be able to decode the message.

NATIONAL CRYPTOLOGIC MUSEUM

Located in Fort Meade, Maryland, the National Cryptologic Museum displays exhibits that bring to life cryptographic artifacts used to encrypt and decrypt secret information throughout history. Visitors are able to view a collection of technological gadgets that have evolved in the use of cryptography and learn about and understand the people and organizations that have been active in using cryptography for both military and civilian use. Exhibits also help to illustrate how valuable cryptography has been to our national security, from our ability to send secret messages to our own military commanders to our capacity to decipher and exploit our enemy's information. The museum also houses a large collection of artifacts that range from rare books and photographs to cipher machines, electronic coding and decoding equipment, cryptographic finds, and more.

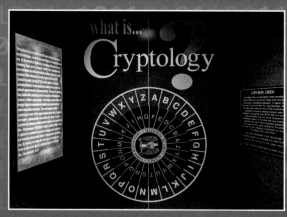

Its location is well known, so are its secrets. The National Cryptologic Museum is an exciting place to visit to learn more about the history of cryptography.

COMMON CODES

There are an infinite number of possible combinations of codes available to use for encrypting information. And there will always be new codes developed. But some codes have become well known and even famous for their use throughout history. Morse code is one popular example.

Another common code was known as the Enigma code. Used heavily during World War II by the Germans, the Enigma code was a way to pass top-secret military messages back and forth between German military commanders and their troops on the ground. It was a sophisticated form of code at the time because it used an Enigma machine, which is similar to a typewriter. The message was typed by using the Enigma machine, but when you pressed a letter on the keyboard a cipher letter would be produced instead. The United States eventually broke the Enigma code and gave the Allies an advantage in the war.

CHAPTER 4

ALGORITHMS

Smartphones come in handy for everything from calling friends and relatives, scheduling doctors appointments, and storing personal contacts to making online purchases, accessing email accounts, and checking account balances on banking apps, just to name a few. Those who use smartphones for work can hold meetings, share private sales data, discuss sensitive business matters, and more. All of this information is private. To keep it that way, smartphones use complex encryption algorithms.

WHAT IS AN ALGORITHM?

In cryptography an algorithm is a sequences of processes, or rules, used to encipher and decipher messages. They are also considered ciphers, which change a message to keep its meaning hidden. Algorithms are complex mathematical sequences and equations that are impossible to complete without computing software. An encryption algorithm is a formula for turning plaintext into encrypted text. In simple terms an algorithm is a set of instructions that take input, such as a message, and provide an output, such as an encrypted message, that changes the data involved in some way.

Many details about our lives are on our phones. Thankfully they are encrypted with complex algorithms that make it nearly impossible to gain access to our sensitive information.

HOW ALGORITHMS WORK WITH KEYS

Encryption algorithms are mathematical formulas or functions that are applied to information to transform it from plaintext into ciphertext. There are two pieces of information an algorithm needs: a key and the plaintext message.

Say you use a ROT-1 cipher to encode a message to a friend. The friend gets the message and, because you told him or her the key, or ROT-1, he or she knows to substitute each letter with the next one in the alphabet. So A becomes B, B becomes C, and so on. Your friend can decode the message, but anyone who finds the message will just see what appears to be a mess of letters. This same principle goes for computer algorithms except on a much larger and more complex scale that is beyond the ability of the human brain to process. Encryption algorithms use much longer and more complex keys to encrypt and decrypt information.

Algorithms carry out calculations by using a series of bits called a key. A binary digit, better know as a bit, is the tiniest component of information in a computer. A bit has a value of 0 or 1. The longer the key, or the more bits it contains, the more combinations it can create, and the harder it is to break the encryption and access the information. AES, or Advanced Encryption Standard, is one type of encryption algorithm. It uses 128-bits, which means there are more than 300,000,000,000,000,000,000,000,000,00 0,000,000 key combinations. Figuring out the right key combination to gain access to the information an AES algorithm is hiding is nearly impossible.

TYPES OF CRYPTOGRAPHIC ALGORITHMS

A cryptographic algorithm is a series of steps performed in a specific sequence by a mathematical calculation to encrypt and decrypt information. There are three different types of cryptographic algorithms: hashing, symmetric key, and asymmetric key.

Symmetric key algorithms, also known as secret key cryptography, use one key for encryption as well as decryption. Using the key, the sender encrypts the plaintext and sends the receiver the ciphertext. Then, using the same key, the receiver decrypts the message and is able to retrieve the plaintext. Both sender and receiver have to know the key for the message if any encryption or decryption is to take place.

Asymmetric key algorithms, or public key cryptography, use a single key to encrypt and another key to decrypt. Public key cryptography is understood by those in cryptography to be the most significant development in the field in nearly four hundred years. Stanford University professor Martin Hellman and his graduate student Whitfield Diffie developed the technique. They wrote a paper in 1976 that described a system that used two keys in which both parties were able to communicate safely without sharing a secret key, even when the channel was not secure. Public key cryptography relies on one-way, easy-to-compute functions, or mathematical functions, whereas the inverse, or opposite, function is challenging to calculate. This system ensures more security in encrypting messages and making sure they stay hidden from unintended audiences.

Using a mathematical transformation, hash functions permanently encrypt data. In other words, the hidden message cannot be deciphered in any way. While it seems counterintuitive to have hidden messages that cannot be decoded, hash functions are used for specific purposes. Passwords, for example, use hash algorithms to verify the person who is logging into an account. A password doesn't need to be deciphered to be used, but a computer system needs to verify that it was entered correctly so access to an email account can be granted. Hash functions are algorithms that ensure data integrity.

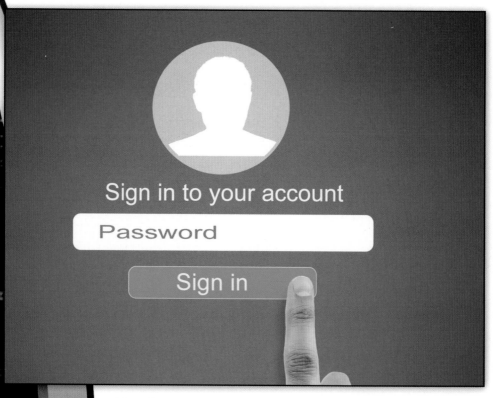

Keeping information safe is the cornerstone of asymmetric key algorithms, which make it increasingly difficult for hackers to gain access to data that requires a log in and password.

FIVE COMMON ENCRYPTION ALGORITHMS

There are five common algorithms that are used widely. They are Triple DES, RSA, Blowfish, Twofish, and AES.

1. **Triple DES,** also known as Triple Data Encryption Algorithm, can be abbreviated as TDEA or Triple DEA. It was created to replace the Data Encryption Standard (DES) algorithm, which was once the standard algorithm used to encrypt electronic information. When hackers learned how to decrypt DES, a new algorithm was needed to replace it. Triple DES uses three separate keys, each with fifty-six bits. That means the total length of the key is 168 bits. More secure and more complex algorithms are slowly replacing triple DES, but it is still widely used throughout the financial services industry.

2. **RSA** is the standard for encrypting data sent over the internet. RSA stands for the first letter of the last names of its three creators, Ron Rivest, Adi Shamir, and Leonard Adleman, who developed the algorithm while working at the Massachusetts Institute of Technology. RSA uses two keys: the first key encrypts a message, and the second key decrypts it. The encrypted content is a mess of unintelligible data that would take a hacker lots of time and massive computing power to decrypt.

3. **Blowfish** is another algorithm designed to replace DES. Blowfish takes messages and splits them into blocks of sixty-four bits, then it encrypts the blocks separately. This algorithm is used to secure e-commerce systems, which allow you to buy products online, as well as to secure passwords. Its creator, Bruce Schneier, who is a computer security expert, did not patent Blowfish. At the time many other encryption algorithms were proprietary or being used by the government. Schneier decided he wanted his algorithm out in the world and available for anyone to use, so he made it free and available on the internet for download.

Bruce Schneier, a computer security specialist, introduced a way for e-commerce sites to encrypt data. He made his program, Blowfish, open source, which means anyone can download and use it.

4. **Twofish** was created by Bruce Schneier, who created Blowfish, and a team that consisted of additional computer security experts. Twofish is a symmetric technique using only one key; however, that key can be up to 256 bits in length. It's extremely fast and, like Blowfish, it is also free and available for download on the internet. Twofish and Blowfish are both excellent encryption algorithms for creating secure environments for hardware and as well as software.

5. **AES,** which stands for Advanced Encryption Standard, is an algorithm that is widely used and trusted by the US government. AES is based on the Rijndael cipher, which is a family of ciphers with different key and block sizes that was developed by two Belgian cryptographers. For AES, three Rijndael ciphers were chosen, each with a block of 128 bits. However, there are three different key lengths: 128-bit key, 192-bit key, and 256-bit key. Because of the three varying key lengths, AES is considered completely resistant to attacks. Security experts anticipate that AES will become the standard used in all industries in the future.

CHAPTER 5

KEYS

I n December 2013, Target Stores experienced an unprecedented breach of security when hackers stole the encrypted personal identification numbers (PINs) of the debit cards of forty million customers at checkout point-of-sale systems located in stores nationwide. Unlike credit card transactions, to use a debit card the user enters a PIN number. This enables a payment from your personal bank account directly to the store. Debit cards provide a direct link to any money in your checking or savings accounts. With your card number and PIN, anyone can access your accounts.

As encryption becomes more sophisticated, so do hackers, who have become ambitious in their attacks on corporations, such as Target, health care companies, and financial institutions.

In the Target hack, the point-of-sale machines where debit cards are swiped were hacked, which enabled the hackers to collect the debit card numbers and PINs. Normally, encrypted data, such as your debit card or credit card number, is useless without a key. But in this incident, hackers gained both the encrypted data and the key, which was the PIN number, to unlock it, giving them potential access to millions of bank accounts everywhere.

The solution to this problem came with chip cards, a new type of credit or debit card that contains an embedded chip that holds a few cryptographic keys and can accomplish several cryptographic processes. Chip cards eliminate the potential for someone to steal a PIN number. During each transaction, the chip creates a specific one-time key

The chip card is the latest in innovative technology that makes it more difficult for hackers to steal your financial information.

assigned to that transaction to secure any data passed between the card and the merchant during the point of sale (such as a credit or debit number and PIN). This is an example of cryptographic keys at work in our daily lives.

WHAT IS A KEY?

In cryptography, a key is a core part of being able to encrypt and decrypt information. For information to remain secret, only the people who are exchanging the information should know a key. A key is a variable that applies an algorithm, which is a complex mathematical equation, to a plaintext message to produce encrypted text or to decrypt text. You can think about a key as the secret piece of information that unlocks encrypted information. Without it, the information is useless.

A BASIC PRINCIPLE OF MODERN CRYPTOGRAPHY: KERCKHOFFS'S PRINCIPLE

Auguste Kerckhoffs, a Dutch linguist and cryptographer who was born in 1835, developed a straightforward principle after studying state-of-the-art military cryptography used at the time by the French military. The idea behind Kerckhoffs's principle is simple: a cryptographic system needs to be secure regardless of whether all the system's information—except the key—is known to the public. His principle outlines six rules for creating secure cryptographic systems. A cryptographic system should be as follows:

1. Indecipherable, even if a hacker gains access to the encrypted message and its algorithm
2. Must not be a secret, so if the message falls into enemy hands, it's less dangerous
3. Must be simple enough to be remembered without the use of written documents
4. Telegraphable, or able to be sent on to the receiver
5. Portable, as in any equipment needed to encrypt or decrypt information should be easy to transport
6. Easy to use

Kerckhoffs's principle is applied in nearly all modern-day encryption algorithms used today.

TYPES OF KEYS

Just as you have different keys for your car, house, and gym locker, there are multiple types of keys that can be used in the world of digital communications. These different keys are based on the type of information that needs to be secured, as well as how the information is encrypted and decrypted.

All keys have one of four properties: symmetric, asymmetric, public, or private. By now you may have guessed how symmetric and asymmetric keys work. Symmetric keys use a single key to both encrypt and decrypt information. Asymmetric keys use one key for encryption and a second key for decryption. Private keys are, as the name implies, private and only known to the people deciphering information. Public keys, as their name also infers, are public and known to everyone.

ATTRACTING HACKERS WITH HONEY

Premera Blue Cross, Chick-fil-A, Sony Pictures, the US Postal Service, The Home Depot—all of these companies, and thousands more, have been hacked, with personal and sensitive information stolen. Right now, the way hackers gain entry into complicated computing systems is to use software that decrypts encrypted data by guessing hundreds of thousands of potential keys. At some point the software hits upon the right key and unlocks a treasure chest of information and data. A team of researchers may have found a way to stop, or at least significantly slow down, hackers. They have created a new type of encryption device where any time an incorrect password or encryption key is guessed, the hackers are sent an incomprehensible mess of information. It's called Honey Encryption. Decoyed data is sent every single time an incorrect password is entered, resulting in millions of pieces of information. If a password is eventually hit upon by the hacking software, the real data is lost amid a sea of unintelligible information.

A popular question in understanding keys is the difference between asymmetric and symmetric keys. You can't talk about keys without talking about algorithms, a mathematical process or formula used to solve a problem. Symmetric key algorithms, which encrypt and decrypt using the same key, are faster and can handle thousands of keys with little computing. The downside is that the key must be sent to the receiver along with the message. This introduces an opportunity for the key to be discovered and the information to be compromised or stolen. Asymmetric keys, which use different keys for encryption and decryption, offer stronger security against theft. The key used to encrypt the data stays with the originator of the message; the receiver uses a second key to decrypt the information on the other end. This process ensures confidentiality, requires authentication by the receiver, and protects against the theft of information.

There are numerous types of keys in cryptography, with each one designed for its own purpose. Following is a selection of common keys used in cryptography:

Authentication key: This key ensures that the integrity of the information and the identity of the sender are dependable and genuine.

Authorization key: These are used to provide access to information. A password to an email account, for example, is an authorization key. The same authorization key (a password, for example) is used by the organization that is responsible for granting access to the information (an email server such as Gmail). Each time a correct password is entered into Gmail for an account, Google authenticates the password as being true and grants access to the user.

RNG key: Short for "random number generation," these are keys used to generate a sequence of random numbers that cannot be predicted. On some websites, when you log in you are assigned a random ID for the time you are active on the site. The ID is randomly generated and unique to you. If someone can guess your random ID number you can be impersonated on that website. There have been incidents of inappropriate comments made on websites by people being impersonated. A group of people was also able to cheat in an online game of poker.

Signature key: The signature key verifies a digital signature. A digital signature is used when signing a digital document. This key verifies that the source of the information, or the signature, is authentic and the documents or information are verifiable.

CRYPTOGRAPHY:
SECURING OUR FUTURE

With the incredible growth of the internet and the vast ways in which we use it, there is plenty of personal information we don't want shared. From credit and debit card information and social security numbers to private communications, passwords, personal details, banking information, and sensitive corporate information, cryptography makes it possible for us to operate within our daily lives and have some measure of security. We can be assured that each time we use our credit card on a website to buy something the account information isn't falling into the wrong hands. Encryption, or the process of encoding and decoding information using algorithms, ciphers, keys,

FBI VERSUS APPLE: SECURITY AND OUR PERSONAL DEVICES

On December 2, 2015, in San Bernardino, California, husband and wife Syed Rizwan Farook and Tashfeen Malik attended a holiday party at the Inland Regional Center, where they proceeded to kill fourteen people and seriously injure another twenty-two in a terrorist attack. Farook and Malik were killed hours later in a gunfight with law enforcement. The Federal Bureau of Investigation located Farook's iPhone and sought assistance from Apple Inc. to help them access the phone. Apple's iPhones have a security feature that will erase all information and data on the phone if ten unsuccessful password attempts are made on the phone. The phone was Farook's employee cell phone, not his personal phone. Investigators have reported that Farook and his wife destroyed both of their personal cell phones prior to the shooting. The FBI wanted

When Apple refused to help the FBI gain access to an iPhone used in a mass shooting, a larger conversation began about privacy laws, encryption, and information security.

(continued on the next page)

(continued from the previous page)

to gain access to Farook's employee phone to see if it contained any evidence of their motivation for the shooting. They reached out to Apple to help them. But Apple said no.

According to an article by Arjun Kharpal, in a statement released to the media Apple chief executive Tim Cook said accessing the phone would require writing new software and that the new software could become "a master key, capable of opening hundreds of millions of locks." Cook's concern lies in offering an access point to a people's private information stored on their phone.

The FBI took the case to court with a federal judge asking Apple to provide some technical assistance to the agency. Apple declined. In the end a private third party was able to gain access to the phone.

The case grew in controversy because it became a high-profile debate between the federal government and a private technology company over encryption and information security and privacy. Law enforcement agencies claim that encryption can make it harder to solve cases or stop terrorist attacks from taking place. Apple and other technology companies have said encryption is necessary to protect user data from hackers looking to steal personal information.

and codes, ensures that our information stays secure as it travels over cyberspace and bounces from one computing network to another.

And as hackers get more sophisticated, so are encryption techniques: encryption has become better at protecting and defending our computing systems against attacks on our personal data and information. Modern cryptography is a fairly young field of study and, with the increasing power of computing systems, there is no telling how sophisticated the field could become.

GLOSSARY

algorithm A series of steps that solve a mathematical problem or that complete a computer process.

bit A unit of information in computing that has only two values, zero or one.

byte A unit of information that consists of eight bits.

cipher A way to hide messages.

cipher alphabet Letters that are substituted for the letters of a standard alphabet.

ciphertext Plaintext that has been encrypted.

code A system of words, letters, figures, or other symbols that are substituted for other words.

confidentiality Keeping information secret or private.

cryptography The art and science of hiding messages.

cryptology The study of encrypting messages.

cybersecurity Steps taken to keep computers and computer systems/networks safe from unauthorized access or hacking attempts.

decryption The process of converting a hidden message into plaintext.

encryption The process of converting plaintext into a hidden message.

iconology The study of visual clues and their symbolism and interpretation.

key A piece of information that is applied using an algorithm to produce encrypted text or to decrypt text.

linguist A person who studies language and its structure.

open source Computer programming that has been made available to anyone to use, for any purpose.

plaintext A text or message that has not yet been encrypted.

principle An idea, belief or theory that forms the basis of something.

standard alphabet The alphabet we use to write the English language.

substitution Replacing one thing for another.

symbolist A person who reads and interprets symbols.

symbology The study and use of symbols.

third party An entity that is in addition to the two primarily parties involved in a situation.

FOR MORE INFORMATION

American Cryptogram Association
56 Sanders Ranch Road
Moraga, CA 94556-2806
Website: http://www.cryptogram.org
The American Cryptogram Association promotes the hobby and art of cryptanalysis, or breaking codes.

Center for Cryptologic History
National Security Agency, Suite 6886
Fort Meade, MD 20755
(301) 688-2336
Website: www.nsa.gov/about/cryptologic_heritage/center_crypt_history
The Center for Cryptographic History maintains historic records and infor- mation on cryptology relating to the decision making of the US intelligence community.

Centre for Applied Cryptographic Research (CACR)
200 University Avenue, W
Waterloo, ON N2L 3G1
Canada
(519) 888-4567
Website: http://cacr.uwaterloo.ca
Operating as a joint project between the University of Waterloo and the Canadian government, the CACR promotes the education of cryptographic

researchers and the application of cryptographic research, especially to the field of information security.

National Cryptologic Museum
9900 Colony Seven Road
Fort Meade, MD 20755
(301) 688-5436
Website: http://cryptologicfoundation.org
The This museum educates the public on the uses and history of cryptography, as well as its value to US preservation and security.

National Security Agency(NSA)
9800 Savage Road, Suite 6248
Fort Meade, MD 20755-6248
(301) 688-6524
Website: www.nsa.gov
The NSA is the leading US government agency that operates and manages our national security using world-class cryptologic systems and tools.

WEBSITES

Because of the changing nature of internet links, Rosen Publishing has developed an online list of websites related to the subject of this book. This site is updated regularly. Please use this link to access the list:

http://www.rosenlinks.com/CCMCB/ciph

FOR FURTHER READING

Barber, Nicola. *Who Broke The Wartime Codes?* Portsmouth, NH: Heinemann, 2015.

Berloquin, Pierre. *Breaking Codes: Unravel 100 Cryptograms.* New York, NY: Sterling, 2014.

Cawthorne, Nigel. *Alan Turing: The Enigma Man.* London, UK: Arcturus Publishing, 2013.

Curley, Rob. *Cryptography: Cracking Codes.* New York, NY: Rosen Publishing Group, 2013.

Durrett, Deanne. *Unsung Heroes of World War II: The Story of the Navajo Code Talkers.* Lincoln, NE: Bison Books, 2009.

Gaines, Helen F. *Cryptanalysis: A Study of Ciphers and Their Solution.* Mineola, NY: Dover Publications, 2014.

Gardner, Martin. *Codes, Ciphers and Secret Writing.* Mineola, NY: Dover Publications, 2013.

Johnson, Bud. *Break the Code: Cryptography for Beginners.* Mineola, NY: Dover Publications, 2013.

Mackay, Jenny. *Cryptology* (Crime Scene Investigations). Farmington Hills, MI: Lucent Books/Greenhaven Press, 2010.

McFadzean, Lesley. *Creating and Cracking Codes.* New York, NY: PowerKids Press, 2013.

Singh, Simon. *The Code Book: The Science of Secrecy from Ancient Egypt to Quantum Cryptography.* Sioux City, IA: Anchor Publications, 2011.

Steele, Kim. *Cryptograms: 269 Cryptoquote Puzzles from History's Most Influential People.* Farmington Hills, MI: Lucent Books/Greenhaven Press, 2014.

Stelle, Kim. *Cryptograms: 269 Entertaining and Enlightening Cryptoquote Puzzles.* New York, NY: Puzzlewright Press/Sterling Publishing Company, 2015.

Weiss, Scott. *Crypto-Lists: Crack the Categorically Clever Codes.* New York, NY: Puzzlewright Press/Sterling Publishing Company, 2016.

Wiese, Jim, and Ed Shems. *Spy Science: 40 Secret-Sleuthing, Code-Cracking, Spy-Catching Activities for Kids.* Hoboken, NJ: Jossey-Bass, 2009.

BIBLIOGRAPHY

Bradford, Contel. "5 Common Encryption Algorithms and the Unbreakables of the Future." StorageCraft Technology, 2016 (http://www.storagecraft .com/blog/5-common-encryption-algorithms).

"A Brief History of Cryptography." Redhat, March 2016 (https://securityblog .redhat.com/2013/08/14/a-brief-history-of-cryptography).

"Career Profile: Cryptologist." Careers that Don't Suck.com, February 24, 2007 (http://careersthatdontsuck.com/2007/02/24/career-profile-cryptologist).

"Classical Cryptography." The University of Rhode Island, 2016 (https:// www.cs.uri.edu/cryptography/classicaltransposition.htm).

"Cryptographic Key." Techpedia, 2016 (https://www.techopedia.com/ definition/24749/cryptographic-key).

"Definition of Encryption Algorithm." PC Mag, 2016 (http://www.pcmag. com/encyclopedia/term/42595/encryption-algorithm).

Feinberg, Ashley. "Sneaky 'Honey Encryption' Stops Hackers By Drowning Them in Phony Data." Gizmodo, January 29, 2014 (http://gizmodo.com /sneaky-honey-encryption-stops-hackers-by-drowning-the-1511718913).

Hipschman, Ron. "The Secret Language." Exploratorium, 1995 (http:// www.exploratorium.edu/ronh/secret/secret.html).

"Kerckhoffs's Principle." Crypto-IT, 2015 (http://www.crypto-it.net/eng/ theory/kerckhoffs.html).

Kharpal, Arjun. "Apple vs FBI: All You Need to Know." CNBC, March 29, 2016 (http://www.cnbc.com/2016/03/29/apple-vs-fbi-all-you-need -to-know.html).

McCormick, Rich. "Apple VP Says FBI Encryption Order 'Puts Everyone at Risk.'" The Verge, March 6, 2016 (http://www.theverge.com/2016/3/6 /11170710/apple-fbi-vp-software-encryption-order-risk).

Mulcahy, Kate. "10 Codes and Ciphers." Listverse, March 13, 2012 (http://listverse.com/2012/03/13/10-codes-and-ciphers).

Reinholm, James H. "Classification of Cryptographic Keys." Cryptomathic.com, August 26, 2015 (http://www.cryptomathic.com/news-events/blog/classification-or-cryptographic-keys).

Robinson, Rick. "Three Lessons from the Target Hack of Encrypted PIN Data." Security Intelligence, January 9, 2014 (https://securityintelligence.com/target-hack-encrypted-pin-data-three-lessons/).

Schillemat, Brandon. "Has the Code of The Zodiac Killer Been Cracked?" Patch, July 18, 2012 (http://patch.com/california/fostercity/has-the-code-of-the-zodiac-killer-been-cracked).

Shelton, Barry K. "Introduction to Cryptography." Information Security Systems, 2015 (http://www.infosectoday.com/Articles/Intro_to_Cryptography/Introduction_Encryption_Algorithms.htm).

Simpson, Sarah. "Cryptography Defined/Brief History." University of Texas, 1997 (http://www.laits.utexas.edu/~anorman/BUS.FOR/course.mat/SSim/history.html).

"The Verona Project." National Security Agency, 2016 (https://www.nsa.gov/public_info/declass/venona/index.shtml).

Wagenseil, Paul. "Smartphone Encryption: What You Need to Know." Tom's Guide, February 29, 2016 (http://www.tomsguide.com/us/smartphone-encryption-faq,news-21915.html).

Ward, Marc. "How the Modern World Depends on Encryption." BBC News, October 25, 2013 (http://www.bbc.com/news/technology-24667834).

"What Are Codes?" National Security Agency, 2016 (https://www.nsa.gov/kids/ciphers/ciphe00001.shtml).

"What Are QR Codes Used For?" Mobile-QR-codes.org. Retrieved April 4, 2016 (http://www.mobile-qr-codes.org/what-are-qr-codes-used-for.html).

Wilsont, William R. "World War II: Navajo Code Talkers." Historynet, June 12, 2006 (http://www.historynet.com/world-war-ii-navajo-code -talkers.htm).

Woodford, Chris. "Encryption and Steganography." Explain that Stuff, March 17, 2016 (http://www.explainthatstuff.com/encryption.html).

"Zodiac Killer Biography." Biography.com, 2016 (http://www.biography .com/people/zodiac-killer-236027).

About the Author

Laura La Bella is a writer and the author of more than thirty-five nonfiction children's books. She has profiled actress and activist Angelina Jolie in *Celebrity Activists: Angelina Jolie—Goodwill Ambassador to the UN*; reported on the declining availability of the world's fresh water supply in *Not Enough to Drink: Pollution, Drought, and Tainted Water Supplies*; and has examined the food industry in *Safety and the Food Supply*. La Bella lives in Rochester, New York, with her husband and two sons.

Photo Credits

Cover agsandrew/Shutterstock.com; p. 7 tetmc/iStock/Thinkstock; p. 11 Nicholas Kamm/AFP/Getty Images; p. 13 Hulton Archive/Getty Images; pp. 14, 30 Bettmann/Getty Images; p. 17 AF archive/Alamy Stock Photo; p. 19 kprojekt/iStock/Thinkstock; p. 23 Encyclopaedia Britannica /Universal Images Group/Getty Images; p. 26 Zhang Peng/LightRocket /Getty Images; p. 28 roxanabalint/iStock/Getty Images; p. 29 Stockbyte/Thinkstock; p. 32 Zuma Press, Inc./Alamy Stock Photo; p. 35 PabloBenitezLope/iStock/Thinkstock; p. 38 Manuel Faba Orte-ga/iStock/Thinkstock; p. 40 Attila Kisbenedek/AFP/Getty Images; p. 42 John Greim/LightRocket /Getty Images; p. 43 Ulrich Baumgarten/Getty Images; p. 49 MacFormat Magazine /Future/Getty Images; back cover and interior pages (binary numbers pattern) © iStockphoto.com/Vjom; interior pages (numbers and letters pattern) © iStockphoto.com/maxkabakov.

Designer: Matt Cauli; Editor: Heather Moore Niver; Photo Researcher: Philip Wolny